U.S. Coast Guard Emergency Response and Disaster Operations

Using Social Media for Situational Awareness

DOUGLAS YEUNG, SARAH A. NOWAK, SOHAELA AMIRI, AARON C. DAVENPORT, EMILY HOCH, KELLY KLIMA, COLLEEN M. MCCULLOUGH

APPROVED FOR PUBLIC RELEASE; DISTRIBUTION UNLIMITED.

Published in 2020

Preface

Researchers from the Homeland Security Operational Analysis Center (HSOAC) conducted a research study on the feasibility of using social media information to aid U.S. Coast Guard (USCG) response operations. The aim of this project was to contribute to the mission of the U.S. Department of Homeland Security (DHS) to ensure resilience to disasters by helping DHS understand whether and how social media might be better leveraged to improve situational awareness during response operations. The HSOAC team found that, for decades, the USCG and other boaters have relied on communication channels that are intended specifically for maritime safety. As such, these channels provide specific information that can be used to locate mariners in distress. Yet we also found that a significant proportion of distress calls now come to the USCG through other means, such as cell phones and, indirectly, from 911 calls. This raises several concerns about potential hindrances to the USCG's search-and-rescue mission, including lack of location information, uncertainty about overwater cell coverage, and lack of organizational capacity to collect and analyze social media information. Informed by these findings, we recommend that DHS develop policies and procedures to facilitate sharing cell phone distress location data with the USCG, that the USCG work to ensure that an organization—itself or another—assumes responsibility for understanding cell coverage over water, and that the USCG identify other missions in which social media information could help increase maritime safety and security and enhance environmental protection and response operations. Although the primary focus of this research was response operations of the USCG, we anticipate that the findings and recommendations could hold benefits for other mission sets of the USCG, such as prevention-oriented missions. Additionally, we anticipate benefit for other components of the DHS enterprise that conduct response operations—principally, the Federal Emergency Management Agency and the U.S. Secret Service.

This research was sponsored by the USCG and conducted within the Strategy, Policy, and Operations Program of the HSOAC federally funded research and development center (FFRDC).

About the Homeland Security Operational Analysis Center

The Homeland Security Act of 2002 (Section 305 of Public Law 107-296, as codified at 6 U.S.C. § 185) authorizes the Secretary of Homeland Security, acting through the Under Secretary for Science and Technology, to establish one or more FFRDCs to provide independent analysis of homeland security issues. The RAND Corporation operates HSOAC as an FFRDC for DHS under contract HSHQDC-16-D-00007.

The HSOAC FFRDC provides the government with independent and objective analyses and advice in core areas important to the department in support of policy development, decisionmaking, alternative approaches, and new ideas on issues of significance. The HSOAC FFRDC also works with and supports other federal, state, local, tribal, and public- and private-sector organizations that make up the homeland security enterprise. The HSOAC FFRDC's research is undertaken by mutual consent with DHS and is organized as a set of discrete tasks. This report presents the results of research and analysis conducted under task 70RSAT18FR0000127, Integration of Social Media and Response Operations.

The results presented in this report do not necessarily reflect official DHS opinion or policy.

For more information on HSOAC, see www.rand.org/hsoac. For more information on this publication, see www.rand.org/t/RR4296.

Contents

Figures and Tables

Figures

Tables

Summary

Social media can play multiple roles in response operations, including enhancing situational awareness, meaning that they can be used to provide access to information that translates to actionable cues in a timely fashion to facilitate effective and efficient decisionmaking. But using social media poses several challenges. The aim of this project was to contribute to the mission of the U.S. Department of Homeland Security (DHS) to ensure resilience to disasters by helping DHS understand whether and how social media might be better leveraged to improve situational awareness during response operations. The primary focus of this research was response operations of the U.S. Coast Guard (USCG). To accomplish these tasks, we performed several types of analyses. First, to examine the social media tools currently used to improve situational awareness during disaster response operations, we conducted interviews with stakeholders and briefly reviewed academic literature on how social media data have been used in the past to gather information that could be relevant to situational awareness during response operations. We also reviewed after-action and lessons-learned reports from recent USCG documents, such as mission analysis reports. Second, we conducted semistructured interviews about social media use with subject-matter experts from the USCG and other government and nongovernment agencies involved in disaster response. Third, we analyzed search-and-rescue (SAR) data from the Marine Information for Safety and Law Enforcement (MISLE) database as an independent source of evidence to help identify current challenges in USCG SAR operations.

Key Findings

Through this research, we aimed to explore the use of social media in response operations, such as the extent to which existing social media aggregation and information extraction tools can help to improve situational awareness during such operations. In addition, the report describes current challenges that could constrain the USCG's ability to effectively use social media for these operations.

For decades, the USCG and other boaters have relied on communication channels (e.g., marine VHF-FM Channel 16 international distress frequency[1]) that are intended specifically for maritime safety. As a result, these channels provide specific information that can be used to locate mariners in distress. However, we found that a significant proportion of distress calls now come to the USCG through other means, such as cell phones and, indirectly, from 911 calls. This introduces constraints that can hinder the USCG's SAR mission performance, including lack of location information, uncertainty about overwater cell coverage, and lack of organizational capacity to collect and analyze social media information.

Recommendations

With these findings, we offer several recommendations that could help inform the development of social media tools the USCG could use in SAR operations and emergency first responder operations. These include, for example, a tool that illustrates a common operating picture (COP) to visually locate assets and people in distress. Another use of these recommendations would be to modify USCG guidance and policies on the use of social media in response operations. The USCG might be able to implement some of these recommendations directly; implementation of others will require working with partners.

Specific recommendations include the following. First, we recommend that DHS **develop policies and procedures to facilitate**

---

[1]   *VHF* stands for very high frequency. *FM* stands for frequency modulation.

sharing cell phone distress location data with the USCG. Interviewees suggested that a significant proportion of distress calls received and communications with mariners in distress will not include location information, whether those are 911 calls in which location information is not shared either with law enforcement or with the USCG or direct calls made with cell phones. The unavailability of location information for someone in distress constrains the USCG's ability to assist them. Developing procedures that enable members of the public to share global positioning system locations from cell phones if they are in distress could help remedy this. Several location-sharing options could help—a messaging app, a mapping app, a dedicated app, and a web browser. The USCG could start by implementing the messaging and mapping app options almost immediately, by relying on apps that people are likely to have already. The other option could require (1) obtaining approval for software that enables text messaging from computers so that the USCG could send messages to those who have called for assistance; (2) allowing access to websites to which the most-common navigation apps (e.g., Google Maps) link, so that USCG command centers could open links sent to them; and (3) developing basic guides that someone in a command center could use to walk a caller through how to send a location if they are unfamiliar.

Second, we recommend that the USCG **work to ensure that an organization—either itself or another—assumes responsibility for understanding cell coverage over water.** Cell phones have become critical to the USCG SAR mission and are likely to remain so in the foreseeable future. However, the USCG has no responsibility or insight into what current cellular coverage is or about the long-term risks in relying on cellular phones to do the SAR mission. As a result, the USCG does not have reliable information about where there might be cellular coverage over bodies of water, either to inform its own missions or to share with mariners. The USCG bears responsibility for maintaining certain radio frequencies and systems a certain distance from shore, but it does not appear that any organization is deliberately monitoring, overseeing, or advocating cellular coverage over water. The USCG could seek to directly collect coverage information by conducting tests of cell phone signals at different distances from shore by deployed assets and should also consider advocating that it or another organization be responsible for maintaining oversight of cellular coverage over water.

Third, we recommend that the USCG **identify other missions in which social media information could help to increase maritime safety and security and enhance environmental protection and response operations** (e.g., reporting environmental hazards, such as oil spills). Although the primary focus of this research was the USCG's response operations, the findings and recommendations could hold benefits for other USCG mission sets, such as prevention-oriented missions. Social media capabilities could also be useful to support marine casualty investigations and civil investigations relating to this regulatory mission, which the USCG considers a prevention mission rather than response operations. Passive monitoring of social media activity could also help the USCG gain awareness of events affecting maritime safety or security (e.g., protests, facility strikes, large marine events).

Acknowledgments

We thank our project sponsor and multiple subject-matter experts at the U.S. Coast Guard, each of whom provided invaluable guidance and information. Experts at other disaster response organizations provided similarly valuable information. RAND colleagues Elizabeth L. Petrun Sayers and Luke J. Matthews reviewed an earlier draft of this report, and Michelle D. Ziegler and former Coast Guard fellow CAPT Jonathan Theel provided advice and feedback. Lance Tan, Erica Robles, and Stephanie Bingley provided administrative assistance throughout the project. Paul S. Steinberg improved the clarity and organization of this report.

Abbreviations

CGD	U.S. Coast Guard district
DHS	U.S. Department of Homeland Security
DOT	U.S. Department of Transportation
DSC	digital selective calling
ESF	emergency support function
FCC	Federal Communications Commission
FEMA	Federal Emergency Management Agency
FFRDC	federally funded research and development center
FM	frequency modulation
FY	fiscal year
GPS	global positioning system
HSOAC	Homeland Security Operational Analysis Center
MAR	mission analysis report
MISLE	Marine Information for Safety and Law Enforcement
nm	nautical mile
R21	Rescue 21
SAR	search and rescue

SME   subject-matter expert

USCG   U.S. Coast Guard

VHF   very high frequency

CHAPTER ONE

Introduction

Background

Social Media Can Play Multiple Roles in Response Operations

The use of social media in daily life has grown substantially in the past decade. A 2019 Pew Research poll found that more than 70 percent of Americans use social media to connect with one another (Pew Research Center, 2019). As the user base has grown larger, it has also grown more representative of the broader population; for example, 69 percent of 50- to 54-year-olds reported that they regularly engaged with at least one platform—primarily Facebook (Pew Research Center, 2019). One such use of social media is to share critical information in emergencies. For instance, researchers conducting a 2012 American Red Cross study found that 40 percent of respondents would use social media to tell others they were safe, as is seen on Facebook after mass shootings (American Red Cross, 2012).

During disasters, social media can be used in several ways by both the public and responding organizations. Individuals can post pictures of disaster conditions or send calls for help. Disaster response organizations can use social media to enhance situational awareness—that is, to provide access to information that translates to actionable cues in a timely fashion to facilitate effective and efficient decisionmaking. Organizations responding to disasters need to know how to quickly locate affected areas and people and to allocate response resources accordingly. Given this, situational awareness is crucial for effective disaster response operations. Because social media are typically public, are frequently updated, and are often location-specific, they can provide a wealth of potentially valuable information. Social media can be used for risk and hazard analysis, such as estimating damage based on calls for help or pictures of an affected area.

One recent example of an organization using social media in disaster response for situational awareness is the U.S. Coast Guard (USCG), which uses social media before, during, and after a disaster. For instance, as the 2018 Subtropical Storm Alberto approached the Gulf Coast, both the Federal Emergency Management Agency (FEMA) and USCG social media outlets disseminated tailored communications to the public, thus establishing lines of social media communication during disaster response and providing situational awareness for first responders and communities at risk. The USCG uses multiple social media platforms to do this, including its Facebook, YouTube, Instagram, Flickr, and WordPress accounts.

Social media can be used to field calls for help, similar to 911 calls. During several hurricanes in 2017, social media were, in some instances, the only way for survivors to request assistance. The USCG established a call center based in Washington, D.C., to monitor tagged social media requests. Requests that arrived via social media and by phone were triaged by urgency of need and validated when possible before being routed to operations centers in Texas. The USCG, although it requested that people call 911 instead of posting on social media, also set up impromptu capabilities to handle social media calls for help.

Social media data can also be used to respond to disasters by facilitating force coordination, relief provision, psychological or medical assistance, and cleanup coordination. This is important because, as Earl McKinney explained, disaster response involves urgent decisionmaking that is irrevocable and based on a solid understanding of the situation, including incomplete or questionable information (McKinney, 2009, p. 42). In disaster response, social media platforms have been used to connect the members of a community. They have also facilitated the aggregation of medical or financial support to disaster-inflicted communities. Additionally, response organizations can tap into this resource to be able to better coordinate their support and relief provision.

Academic research describes common approaches to gathering, processing, and analyzing social media data for disaster response and situational awareness. Twitter is a particularly well-studied disaster response platform because it is broadly used and provides equal opportunity, ease, and timeliness of content-sharing. Disaster types that are often studied include earthquake, flood, tsunami, hurricane, wildfire, and radiation release. For instance, Peter Landwehr and his colleagues described the strength and limitations of Twitter for use in disaster response and identified several features needed to make it more capable in assisting with planning, warning, and support during disasters (Landwehr et al., 2016). Geographic information (spatial and temporal) is often used in case studies of social media for disaster response (Reuter and Kaufhold, 2018). Typically, images that are shared on social media, along with qualitative descriptions of disaster instances, include information on the geographic location that can be harnessed for disaster response (Tim et al., 2017). Additionally, these qualitative posts can contain information about need in times of disaster. Thus, another category of information that has been aggregated and widely used in disaster response is information on rescue needs; missing people; or food, water, and electricity scarcity. Researchers have also highlighted social media's communication functions, emphasizing that information collection and sharing should be supplemented by validation with traditional media sources to verify the reliability and accuracy of social media data (see, e.g., Reuter and Kaufhold, 2018).

The Use of Social Media for Situational Awareness Can Be Challenging

Despite the ongoing use of social media in such circumstances, effectively using social media for situational awareness remains challenging. For some agencies, such as the USCG, using response teams to monitor social media feeds can be labor-intensive, potentially diverting critical human resources from the response efforts themselves. Furthermore, because of the sheer volume of social media posts, those monitoring social media feeds can find it difficult to see all the relevant information that is posted. There is not an established, consistent, and efficient process for first responders to leverage perishable information that is readily available from social media sources. One of the greatest impediments is current U.S. Department of Homeland Security (DHS) policy on the use of social media in response operations, which is very restrictive, primarily because of information security concerns and the overall leadership risk tolerance of publicly accessible media (DHS, 2012). For example, because of this low risk tolerance, many Coast Guard operations centers do not have access to the open internet.

There are also broader challenges to making use of social media data. Large amounts of data can be gathered from social media, which must be organized and processed, and frequently also integrated with data from more-traditional or authoritative sources, such as environmental sensors or satellite data. Organizations in charge of disaster response may need to develop and manage specific data processing and integration mechanisms.

Maintaining data quality is another such challenge (Beath et al., 2012; Kiron, Prentice, and Ferguson, 2014). This includes, for instance, reducing the uncertainty in social media content. It can be difficult to identify and deal with inaccurate, misleading, or redundant data, especially in large volume. Identifying and dealing with shortcomings in technological infrastructure also cannot be overlooked in that it can fall outside the technological capacity of a given organization in charge; an internet outage can completely impede the use of social media in disasters. In addition to ensuring data quality, another challenge for use of social media data in disaster response is to address ethical, legal, and regulatory issues relating to privacy and data security, ownership and security of data sharing, and accountability and responsibility for monitoring online data (Marcellino et al., 2017).

Objective and Approach

An improved understanding of how social media access could be helpful—and where it might not be helpful—could inform future policy on social media in response operations. The aim of this project was to contribute to DHS's mission to ensure resilience to disasters by helping DHS understand whether and how social media might be better leveraged to improve situational awareness during response operations—specifically for the USCG, one of DHS's component agencies that performs response operations daily. These considerations include the organizational constraints on using social media in this way, such as identifying whether populations who do not use social media might be left out or not covered by this capability or be missing out on a potentially valuable information mode that could be systematically leveraged to aid in response and recovery operations as a secondary or redundant source, particularly when conventional means become unavailable.

To address this overall aim, our specific objectives were to do the following:

- Identify the social media aggregators and data extraction tools currently used in disaster response operations.
- Understand how the tools are currently being used, including what types of information users monitor with the tools and how the tools fit into the command-and-control structure of response operations.
- Identify challenges or gaps with the tools from the users' perspective.

To address these questions, we performed several types of analyses. First, to examine the social media tools currently used to improve situational awareness during disaster response operations, we conducted interviews with stakeholders, such as representatives from DHS and other national, state, and local organizations engaged in disaster response. We also briefly reviewed academic literature on how social media data have been used in the past to gather information that could be relevant to situational awareness during response operations. To identify current informational challenges in situational awareness in DHS response operations, we reviewed after-action and lessons-learned reports from recent USCG documents, such as mission analysis reports (MARs).

Second, we conducted semistructured interviews with subject-matter experts (SMEs) from the USCG involved in search-and-rescue

(SAR) operations and from other government and nongovernment agencies involved in disaster response. (The interview protocol can be found in Appendix A.) FEMA's National Response Framework Emergency Support Function (ESF) provides the structure for interagency coordination for a federal response to an incident (e.g., communication or public health) (FEMA, 2019b). As a result, it provides useful background on the multitude of roles required for emergency response and situational awareness, as well as indicating which agencies are involved. For instance, it includes information on where the USCG might be called on to play either a lead or support role. Armed with the ESF information, we reached out to SMEs at federal and state agencies to learn about how they were using social media in response operations. In addition, we spoke with state, local, and private-sector partners to identify areas in which the USCG could leverage external tools and processes. Table 1.1 lists the agencies whose personnel we interviewed and the number of people with whom we spoke from each agency. To identify themes from the interviews, we used a data abstraction table to identify whether agencies used similar social media platforms and analytic tools, what methods they used for compiling and analyzing information, and whether they found value added from using social media data.

Table 1.1
Interviews with Emergency Response Subject-Matter Experts

Entity	People Interviewed	Monitors Social Media?
Centers for Disease Control and Prevention	1	Yes
U.S. Department of Transportation (DOT)	1	Yes
Maryland Governor's Office of Homeland Security	1	Yes
Association of Public-Safety Communications Officials	2	No
California Governor's Office of Emergency Services	2	Yes
Los Angeles Fire Department	1	Yes
Maryland National Guard	2	Yes
Team Rubicon	1	Yes

Third, we analyzed SAR data from the Marine Information for Safety and Law Enforcement (MISLE) database as an independent source of evidence to help identify current challenges in USCG SAR operations. We analyzed MISLE data from fiscal year (FY) 2012 to FY 2018.

Organization of This Report

In Chapter Two, we discuss the ways in which social media are being used in emergency response and disaster operations. Chapter Three describes challenges that might constrain the USCG's abilities to advance its use of social media to aid in response operations. Finally, Chapter Four suggests several recommendations to address these challenges.

This report also includes two appendixes: Appendix A contains the interview protocol we used, and Appendix B contains more detail on the methods we used for the MISLE analyses.

CHAPTER TWO

How Are Social Media Being Used in Emergency Response and Disaster Operations?

Smartphones and mobile applications (commonly referred to as apps) could change the nature of how emergency response organizations gain situational awareness during disasters, such as establishing and maintaining communications. For instance, what information is available from apps or social media? How might these communication channels change the role of the command center as the hub of communications and operations? How might smartphone and cellular communications change overall SAR unit operations and the command center role?

In our interviews, local law enforcement personnel and other emergency responders told us that they found value in social media. These were groups that were equipped with appropriate tools, such as the ability to reach platforms (e.g., Twitter, Facebook) on local workstations, and were encouraged to do so by upper leadership. Several cited the influence of FEMA's Emergency Management Institute, which strongly advocated social media as a situational awareness enhancer. Targeted searches of social media platforms were preferred over aggregators, such as Sysomos, because of the need for greater speed and accuracy than available tools provide.

This chapter discusses several ways in which public- and private-sector organizations currently use social media to assist in emergency response and disaster operations. In it, we describe common ways in which disaster response agencies use social media for situational awareness.

Developing a Common Operating Picture of Ongoing Events

Crowdsourced data, such as from social media, can provide cost-effective, real-time insight into ongoing incidents. Social media also offers new opportunities for data collection—for instance, because of local social media users, this information can also come from places that were once hard to reach. Social media can also help evaluate ongoing response operations in real time, such as identifying rumors or misinformation, and increase awareness of citizen responses and mobilization.

Response organizations have developed multiple ways to collect such crowdsourced information. For instance, FEMA built a smartphone app with several data-collection functions that allow it to support situational awareness. The Disaster Reporter feature allows FEMA to crowdsource photographs and descriptions of disaster areas. In addition to supporting situational awareness, the FEMA app has public affairs functions. It can be used to share emergency notifications, locate emergency shelters, and receive safety tips. In producing its own crowdsourced mobile application, FEMA maintains control over content. By amplifying its data with satellite imagery, it can passively observe social media to strengthen situational awareness (e.g., learning about localized power outages). Similarly, the Virtual Port project of the Port of Long Beach analyzes geolocated social media posts to enhance domain awareness of the port complex, such as the region, coastline, and critical infrastructure. In both situations, the passive observation of social media allows the agency to collect information without actively engaging social media users in a way that might violate privacy or the agency's social media policies. State departments of homeland security similarly monitor social media posts in which content (e.g., hashtags) or embedded location information suggest their relevance for situational awareness at large public gatherings (e.g., parades or festivals). Although continuous monitoring of social media activity can be prohibitively resource-intensive, social media can be a useful asset for timely warnings in bounded instances, such as during disasters.

Interviewees from public health agencies said that they use social media to amplify their knowledge of emerging crises, with leadership briefed daily on these efforts. Manual searches and aggregator tools are used to identify the public's questions and concerns and, at times, rumors and false information. An added benefit is the opportunity to examine, in near-real time, how public messaging, either from social or traditional media, is received.

According to an interviewee from Team Rubicon, a nongovernmental disaster response organization with a volunteer base that relies heavily on military veterans, the organization has taken a manual approach to analyzing social media information for situational awareness. During disasters, Team Rubicon uses a Virtual Operations Support Team to monitor mass media and social media, such as following known Twitter hashtags (Porter, 2018). It also uses crowdsourcing: Remote volunteers scrape social media and compile information into a shared database (e.g., posting in a dedicated social media thread).

Yet the lack of a common operating picture between ESF partners was a recurring theme across our agency interviews, which suggested that each agency develops its own social media monitoring policy and shares the findings in an ad hoc manner. For example, DOT combines Waze and Periscope feeds with Rand McNally mapping software to determine the size of truck that could travel down an isolated road. During emergency activations, DOT shares results at national and regional response coordinating centers. Courses at FEMA's Emergency Management Institute have also been integral to agencies promoting social media use and could be a forum to unify practices and policies.

Receiving Distress Calls and Calls for Aid

Social media can be used to receive messages (e.g., phone calls) and posts about people in distress or areas in need of aid. As seen in the 2017 hurricane season, these can be either messages that people in distress, for example, send directly to the USCG or general postings about a need for assistance, given the frequently public nature of social media. The result is a two-way communication opportunity for organizations to directly engage with those affected by disasters and to broadcast messages to wider audiences as needed.

Yet none of the experts we interviewed felt comfortable receiving distress calls for aid over social media. Whereas many recognized the public's growing use of social media, such as in previous emergencies when other communication lines were unavailable, none felt that they had the resources to receive, process, and respond to calls for aid quickly enough. They did not have sufficient personnel to monitor social media channels continuously or the technology to quickly aggregate inquiries. Furthermore, each interviewee expressed concern about possible erroneous reports. Although the 911 system routinely receives false and incorrect reports,[1] interviewees reported believing that such false or incorrect reports could be more frequent in social media. To deal with potentially inaccurate information, the Sacramento County Office of Emergency Services has proposed a decision matrix that incorporates social media into a traditional incident command system hierarchy. This system permits validation and allows a variety of parties, from public affairs officers to trained volunteers, to monitor and transmit social media calls for support.

Facilitating Interagency Coordination

Awareness of other response activities is a critical component of maintaining overall situational awareness during a disaster (Moroney et al., 2013). In particular, this requires knowing what other response organizations are doing. The USCG at the Ports of Los Angeles and Long Beach, for instance, uses social media for this type of situational awareness. Increased awareness of other organizational response efforts affords additional opportunities to coordinate among organizations.

Law enforcement and other agencies with public safety mandates have used social media to educate themselves on response efforts and to synchronize public affairs messages. Despite having a sophisticated coordination protocol, interviewees cited the process of reviewing partners' social media pages as a quick way to learn about already-activated emergency response. One interviewee reported that, regardless of other infrastructure, the fastest way to learn about a local emergency was to check the local Twitter feeds.

---

[1] Specific data are unavailable.

CHAPTER THREE

Current Challenges in Coast Guard Search-and-Rescue Operations

In this chapter, we first discuss the USCG's Guard's SAR operations and then examine some challenges that might constrain the USCG's abilities to advance its use of social media to aid in response operations.

Coast Guard Search-and-Rescue Operations

The USCG is the primary agency responsible for maritime, coastal, and waterborne SAR operations that require a coordinated federal response (DHS, 2016). It performs all operations necessary to locate, rescue, and aid distressed people while coordinating with emergency managers at the international, national, local, state, tribal, and territorial levels. In noncrisis operations, the primary ways for mariners to submit distress calls to the USCG are global maritime safety and distress systems, digital selective calling (DSC), the National Distress and Response System (very high–frequency [VHF] radio), and cellular phone. Several of these systems are available only to large boats and ships; captains of small boats are most likely to request assistance through VHF radio or cellular phone. As of 2013, the USCG encouraged the use of VHF radio as the primary method of distress notification (USCG, 2013). VHF radios allow for broadcast notification to other boats in the area, for easy direction finding, and for mariners to easily receive urgent broadcasts. However, VHF frequency modulation (FM) range is limited to line of sight or to the VHF antenna heights of the transmitting and receiving stations.

The USCG is regarded as a world leader in SAR policy and operations. The SAR case sequence of events is initiated by a call for assistance, which is usually a voice call over telephone or radio. The initial notification is regarded as the critical point at which the first responder or SAR mission coordinator (or both) attempts to ascertain from the caller the nature of the distress, the degree of danger, location, the vessel identification, the number of people affected, and what safety equipment is available.

The commandant of the USCG has promulgated an instruction to USCG forces detailing the USCG SAR mission coordinator Maritime Assistance Decision Flow Chart to guide SAR operations and response policy. This includes determining whether the SAR case is emergency or nonemergency and what the most-appropriate actions are, given the totality of the circumstances and risk of property damage, personal injury, and loss of life. Current and forecast environmental conditions on the scene, such as weather and sea conditions, heavily influence the urgency of the response and overall safety risk for both first responders and the mariners seeking assistance.

The evolving nature of communication technologies has created both challenge and opportunity for success in the SAR mission. The near ubiquity of cell phones, for instance, offers an invaluable direct channel to those in distress. And given its widespread use, social media could prove a rich resource for situational awareness of disaster conditions. Yet ensuring cell phone accessibility or sifting through and making sense of the constant stream of social media content requires specific technical and organizational capabilities. SMEs with whom we spoke suggested that the office of the USCG Assistant Commandant for Capability—specifically, the Office of C4 [Command, Control, Communication, and Computers] and Sensors Capabilities (CG-761)—is interested in leveraging social media, but it is unsure how much can be gained, whether cell signals can reach far enough offshore, and whether sufficient funding is available to support new tools. Interviewees from CG-761 indicated three roadblocks to change: (1) As DHS increases its cybersecurity requirements, costs increase and functionality and flexibility decrease; (2) current tools do not exist for the formal or informal use of social media in command posts; and (3) a widespread cultural shift toward adopting social media would be necessary for consistent utilization.

Requests for help have recently evolved from the radio to 911 calls. USCG responses to radio calls can use the Rescue 21 (R21) distress system, which has direction finders, whereas 911 operators sometimes receive amorphous and less-useful location information (USCG, 2013). Advanced technologies that provide global positioning system (GPS) coordinates, such as DSC, are available, but they tend to be used only by professional mariners. Although 911 operators are trained to connect with the USCG as appropriate, such calls are hard to immediately locate on the water and frequently require triangulation. Furthermore, depending on the location, coordinating with 911 centers can be difficult, such as in Sector Long Island Sound, where one region relies on regional centers and another has separate centers in each municipality. In addition to distance from shore, interviewees warned, during emergencies, such as natural disasters, cell signals can be unreliable and government communications are prioritized. Those in need of help might be unable to reach the USCG or other first responders. Furthermore, a lost mariner who cannot identify their position might be able to use their GPS receiver to direct first responders and USCG personnel. The robustness of the 911 system is dependent on state and local authorities, as well as local telecommunication providers. Each public safety answering point can have a different level of technology. None of these factors is within the control of the USCG or other first responders (Gallagher, 2018). Next-generation 911 using internet-based systems will allow people to text or send pictures to public safety answering points, but the rollout has been slow and inconsistent, particularly while local governments await federal funding to support the rollout.

Changes in communication technologies and how they are used will affect the USCG's ability to perform the SAR mission. Understanding how specific communication technologies, including those related to cell phones and social media and other platforms, might be an area in which additional social media capabilities can help.

Challenges in Coast Guard Search-and-Rescue Operations

Lack of Information on Offshore and Overwater Cell Phone Coverage

An underlying challenge to the public's increasing reliance on cell phones is that they depend on service coverage over water. However, there is currently no good source of information that details how far offshore reliable cellular service is available. The Federal Communications Commission (FCC) leases cell tower space and provides maps of Long-Term Evolution coverage for the lower 48 states, but it provides no such coverage map for coastal areas or inland waterways (FCC, 2018). The USCG also lacks cell coverage maps because federal statute requires that it maintain only VHF radio infrastructure for maritime communication. One USCG interviewee mentioned asking FirstNet with AT&T, a communication platform for first responders, for cell coverage data. The interviewee said that FirstNet's priority was to cover land in the lower 48 states and that "supporting shore missions is not part of [its] mission." At the time of our research, we could find no federal agency with a mandate to provide overwater cell phone coverage.

As part of our analysis of MISLE data, we estimated the percentage of cases occurring in areas that might have cell coverage. To do this, we mapped all cases using primary latitude and longitude and used the notification type field (i.e., the method used to report the incident, such as R21, VHF, or telephone) to indicate confirmed cases reported by cell phone. Out of all SAR cases listed in MISLE from FY 2012 to FY 2018, roughly 12,500 (about 10 percent) were confirmed to be reported through cell phone. Of the cases confirmed reported via cell phone, roughly 77 percent had a primary location within 3 nautical miles (nm) of shore; roughly 10 percent had a primary location 3 to 12 nm from shore; and roughly 2 percent had a primary location 12 to 24 nm from shore. This suggests that there might be places offshore where cell service can persist until the edge of the customs contiguous zone (24 nm offshore). However, MISLE does not indicate whether a distress call came from someone on land worried about a vessel that was eventually located in that zone or whether it came from within that zone.

Figure 3.1 shows FY 2018 cases around southern Florida, with graduated shading showing the three distances from shore. Cases reported by cell phone are darkly shaded, with small dots indicating cases in which no lives were lost and larger circles indicating at least one life lost. Cases reported by all other methods (e.g., R21, VHF) are lightly shaded. In FY 2018, 257 cases were reported by cell phone in USCG district (CGD) 7 (Miami), which represented about 8 percent of all cases reported in the district. Of the cases reported by cell phone, 3.9 percent included a fatality, compared with 2.8 percent of cases reported by some other method.

Of all 3,001 SAR cases originating from CGD 7 in FY 2018, roughly 60 percent were within 3 nm of shore, shown as the light gray band labeled "State/federal concurrent jurisdiction" in the figure. This district represents the lower end of the range: Overall, 83 percent of

Figure 3.1
Fiscal Year 2018 Search-and-Rescue Cases in Southern Florida

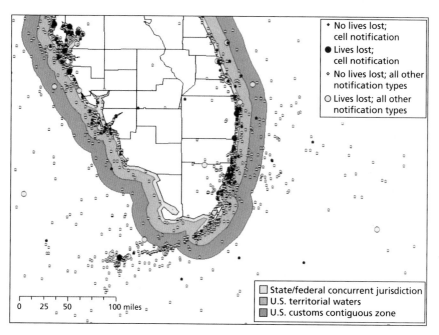

SOURCE: MISLE data.

FY 2018 SAR cases nationwide were within 3 nm of shore. In each of three districts (CGD 7, CGD 1, and CGD 13), more than 90 percent of SAR cases were close to shore.

Figure 3.2 shows the trend over time in the percentage of SAR cases that were closest to shore between FY 2012 and FY 2018. The thickness of the line is proportional to the number of cases in the district for each fiscal year. For all but two districts (7 and 14), more than 60 percent of cases were within 3 nm of shore. With so many cases so close to shore, it is possible that many of them were within areas where existing overland cellular infrastructure extended coverage overwater.

Figure 3.2
Search-and-Rescue Cases Within 3 Nautical Miles of Shore, by Federal Fiscal Year and Originating District

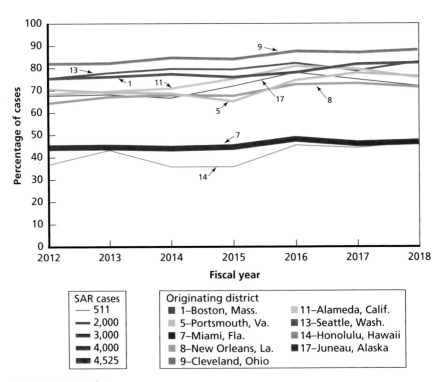

SOURCE: MISLE data.

We were also interested in general patterns in how cases are reported to the USCG. Tables 3.1 and 3.2 show the top ten methods used to contact the USCG for SAR cases opened in district 7 (Miami, Florida) (Table 3.1) and district 9 (Cleveland, Ohio) (Table 3.2) between

Table 3.1
Ten Methods Used Most to Contact the Coast Guard When a Case Was Opened in the Miami, Florida, Originating District (District 7), Fiscal Years 2012 Through 2018

Notification Type	Number of Cases, by Federal Fiscal Year							
	2012	2013	2014	2015	2016	2017	2018	All
Phone call								
Any type to the USCG	1,170	1,297	1,338	1,259	869	924	929	7,786
Cellular to the USCG	515	447	460	437	232	172	247	2,510
911 or other emergency number	332	312	320	376	194	176	169	1,879
R21 or VHF-FM Channel 16								
Data	815	709	789	784	555	639	529	4,820
Voice	405	394	402	393	213	164	178	2,149
SAR satellite-aided tracking, 406 megahertz								
Alone	444	361	387	314	180	174	139	1,999
With E-Solution	48	47	37	48	23	42	33	278
DSC VHF FM	81	83	46	44	36	32	45	367
Other notification method	68	58	57	63	40	52	33	371
Unspecified	342	207	233	310	1,061	740	513	3,406
All	4,525	4,256	4,361	4,277	3,572	3,277	3,001	27,269

SOURCE: MISLE data.

NOTE: The numbers do not add up vertically because the "All" row represents all cases in the district by fiscal year, whereas the rest of the table lists the number of cases reported via the ten most-frequent notification methods. These ten methods account for ~94% of cases in district 7 (Miami) (25,565 ÷ 27,269) and ~96% of cases in district 9 (Cleveland) (17,104 ÷ 17,753) for FYs 2012–2018.

Table 3.2
Ten Methods Most Used to Contact the Coast Guard When a Case Was Opened in the Cleveland, Ohio, Originating District (District 9), Fiscal Years 2012 Through 2018

Notification Type	Number of Cases, by Federal Fiscal Year							
	2012	2013	2014	2015	2016	2017	2018	All
Phone call								
Any type to the USCG	1,266	1,090	1,142	1,298	1,195	1,066	1,068	8,125
Cellular phone call to the USCG	338	186	204	256	297	411	355	2,047
911 or other emergency number	253	139	100	94	131	106	157	980
R21 or VHF-FM Channel 16								
Data	330	335	290	324	313	336	271	2,199
Voice	364	232	162	199	191	143	143	1,434
Waving arms or hand signals	57	33	24	27	30	21	16	208
VHF-FM other than Channel 16	32	12	14	8	10	7	11	94
Other notification method	31	43	19	13	19	22	17	164
None (an assisting unit saw distress)	35	14	18	24	20	33	16	160
Unspecified	242	141	121	131	335	360	363	1,693
All	3,062	2,323	2,159	2,474	2,610	2,596	2,529	17,753

SOURCE: MISLE data.

NOTE: The numbers do not add up vertically because the "All" row represents all cases in the district by fiscal year, whereas the rest of the table lists the number of cases reported via the ten most-frequent notification methods. These ten methods account for ~94% of cases in district 7 (Miami) (25,565 ÷ 27,269) and ~96% of cases in district 9 (Cleveland) (17,104 ÷ 17,753) for FYs 2012–2018.

FY 2012 and FY 2018. These two districts had the highest volumes of SAR cases during this period, with 27,269 total cases in Miami and 17,753 total cases in Cleveland. Of all SAR cases in the Miami district between FY 2012 and FY 2018, 45 percent were reported via telephone, cellular phone, or 911 call; in contrast, 26 percent were reported via R21 or VHF radio. In Cleveland, 63 percent of cases came in by telephone, cellular phone, or 911 call to the USCG; in contrast, only 20 percent of calls came through R21 or VHF radio.

In the two sectors with the most SAR cases, the most frequent method of reporting distress was by telephone and not by the official, federally mandated radio channels the USCG maintains. This was true across the full period of interest and in each of the seven fiscal years for which we had MISLE data; this indicates that the boating public seems to prefer phone calls to radio calls when calling for help.

Lack of Access to the Distress Call Location

Several Coast Guard SMEs pointed to an inability to locate people in distress as one challenge with which social media could help, noting that they would talk to people who were using cell phones with GPS capabilities but whose location the USCG could not determine. MARs and analysis of MISLE data support the SMEs' identification of the problem. They identified two gaps in the MAR: connections with the 911 system and limitations with the R21 system. First, a significant proportion of distress calls to which the USCG responds are indirectly received from the 911 system. There is further supporting evidence about the need for better location information from MISLE. In the data we analyzed from FYs 2012 through 2018, about 40 percent of notifications appear to have been from phones. Most of those likely originated from cell phones, given general statistics about 911 calls (around 80 percent of 911 calls are from cell phones) (National Emergency Number Association, undated). We did not see significant trends over time. A large portion of notification types are unknown, but, in general, it seemed that, for the period we examined, the fraction of all notifications that were radio- or phone-based remained relatively steady.

The problem is that the USCG does not have the same technology that the 911 call centers have. According to the SAR MAR (USCG, 2019), some sectors have outdated phone systems that do not display cell phone location or caller identification. This means that, even if location information is generated when a 911 call comes in, the USCG might not have access to that information. In an interview, USCG SAR SMEs confirmed this to be an issue.

Second, the MARs identified the need to sustain the R21 system. The report on SAR also discusses R21 downtime and the fact that R21 does not always generate a location (USCG, 2019). Two measures from the MISLE data—the number of sorties and sortie outcomes (i.e., failure to locate)—could suggest the difficulty of locating or concern about the difficulty of locating. A larger number of sorties could simply mean that a USCG ship was in the area—that is, this could mean that a crew was close to the suspected location for the SAR case or that the situation was determined to be high risk. The USCG commonly sends multiple units to the location of a distressed mariner, which results in multiple sorties. The USCG standard is to have some asset (including state, local, or commercial assets or other mariners) on the scene within two hours (U.S. Government Accountability Office, 2017).

A caller's location might also be known at the time of the call but shift with changing conditions. The USCG uses drift models to predict the effect of wind and current on mariners' locations, but these models might not be accurate. We did not see large differences in either of these two measures by notification type or distance from cell tower, with an obvious exception. The rate of failure to locate is low for direct visual notification methods—that is, if the notification was that USCG personnel saw someone in distress, they can usually find the distressed party. The implication is that failure to locate a mariner in distress is associated with a potential loss of property, personal injury, or loss of life. The causality likely goes both ways, but it presents at least circumstantial evidence that having better or faster access to location information could ultimately save property or lives.

Lack of Capabilities to Leverage Emerging Communication Technology

Developing analytic capacity for social media data or other emerging communication technologies requires a broad set of capabilities. These include both technical requirements, such as tools and infrastructure, and organizational capacity—that is, creating the conditions that make such analysis feasible.

Technical and Infrastructure Challenges

Emergency services and response organizations can be limited in terms of both resources and technical infrastructure available to them. The ESFs provide the structure for coordinating federal interagency support for a federal response to an incident. They are the mechanisms for grouping functions most frequently used to provide federal support to states and federal-to-federal support, both for declared disasters and emergencies under the Stafford Act and for non–Stafford Act incidents (FEMA, 2019a). We interviewed active and former representatives of several of these agencies. After incidents in which authorities provided updates via social media and members of the public attempted to use social media to identify the suspects (like with the Boston Marathon bombing), social media capabilities were no longer considered an optional tool. Interviewees differed on whether social media was most useful as a tool for data collection, public communication, or both. There is promise in using automated systems, such as algorithms for search terms, but it is possible that no system marketed to ESF partners is sufficiently sensitive or fast, let alone within government budgets. For example, one automated system took at least 24 hours to report positive signals—too late to act on reported information. Furthermore, automated systems cannot differentiate between relevant information and sarcasm or jokes.

Nor has infrastructure caught up with the technology or need. According to an interviewee, one agency purchased 20 months of tweets to retroactively test whether it could monitor Twitter traffic for themes, emerging issues, rumors, or misinformation. However, the agency lacked the computing and human capacity to actually process the information. Also, quickly identifying keywords for aggregators to target is a time-consuming task that might not be feasible during an emerging crisis. Analysis of image-based tools has been more event-driven: Agencies do not have a way to systematically analyze imagery.

Social media were also used for investigative purposes, including passive data collection and learning about specific people. Law enforcement agencies use aggregators, such as TweetDeck and Sysomos to monitor large public gatherings and the risk of protest. Both USCG documentation (USCG, 2013) and interviewees suggested that social media enhance SAR, often providing pertinent information, such as the make and model of a vessel, pictures of missing people, and possible routes.[1] Despite concerns about duplicate reporting, false events, and nonemergencies, one emergency communication interviewee mentioned that the incidence of false social media reporting did not differ from rates of false reporting via 911 calls. Thus, processing social media data presents a significant challenge. Although large amounts of data are available, they must be organized, analyzed, and sufficiently validated in order to be actionable.

Lack of Current Policies and Authorities on Coast Guard Use of Social Media

Potential challenges that social media pose include legal issues that relate to privacy, ownership, and data security, as well as accountability and responsibility for using online data. This goes hand in hand with the challenge of verifying the accuracy and reliability of social media data and data quality in general. The USCG does not have a specific process for using social media in response operations; this is likely partly because of DHS's restrictive policies on using social media (DHS, 2012).

In comparison, the 2011 *U.S. Army Social Media Handbook* lays out standards for soldiers and officers, as well as several case studies (Office of the Chief of Public Affairs, 2011). Although many of its examples remain relevant, it is important to note that social media use rapidly evolving technologies and that many current tools and utilities are not discussed in it. The handbook's checklist for operations security for official pages offers replicable guidelines for public affairs officers and metrics to measure message penetration. The Army recommends that, in crises, one use social media to answer questions, share information, and encourage observers to send information.

---

[1]   Interviews with USCG SAR SMEs conducted between May and August 2019 (see Appendix A for the interview protocol).

Organizational and Cultural Challenges for Use of Social Media

For social media data to be used effectively for disaster response, an organization's staff, especially its leadership, need to understand, value, and support such initiatives. A cultural bias toward relying on existing workflows or training could inhibit innovation and the adoption of new tools. Several interviewees expressed concern about their social media channels being used to propagate false information. Yet simply reverting back to existing procedures, requiring the 911 system to validate all calls, might not provide the desired validity. Frequently, 911 centers are recipients of disinformation, such as prank calls or swatting (the false reporting of an emergency, where no emergency exists, to public safety officials in order to provoke a response from special weapons and tactics personnel) (911.gov, 2015).

To mitigate potential biases that render certain population groups less visible, such as those who might not use social media, people who staff response command centers need to be aware of changing demographics, communication styles, and evolving methods to reach populations where they are. Emergency response experts we interviewed said that they envisioned future social media tools that could automatically collect and identify useful indicators and their reach. As trust in traditional media erodes, agencies might struggle to communicate to the public and ensure that their messages are heard. DHS established a social media working group that has made recommendations on social media messaging in disasters (DHS, 2018). For instance, using social media as a public affairs tool, social media managers can frequently publish updates to help promote transparency and control messaging. Information should be free of ambiguity and double-verified when possible. Central repositories of messages sent and received can be used to monitor rumors, which can be disputed with links, images, or videos from reputable sources (e.g., news agencies).

CHAPTER FOUR

Conclusion and Recommendations

With this report, we have aimed to explore the use of social media in response operations—in particular, the extent to which existing social media aggregation and information extraction tools can help to improve situational awareness during response operations. In addition, we have described current challenges that could constrain the USCG's ability to effectively use social media for response operations.

For decades, the USCG and other boaters have relied on communication channels that are intended specifically for maritime safety (e.g., R21). As such, these channels provide specific information that can be used to locate mariners in distress. Yet we found that a significant proportion of distress calls now come to the USCG through other means, such as cell phones and, indirectly, from 911 calls. This raises concerns about potential hindrances to the USCG's SAR mission, including lack of location information, uncertainty about overwater cell coverage, and lack of organizational capacity to collect and analyze social media information.

Using these findings, we offer several recommendations that could help inform the development of social media tools the USCG could use in SAR operations and emergency first responder operations; these include, for example, a tool that illustrates a common operating picture to visually locate assets and people in distress. Another use of these recommendations would be to modify USCG guidance and policies on the use of social media in response operations. The USCG might be able to implement some of these recommendations directly; implementing others will require working with partners.

Recommendation 1: Develop Policies and Procedures to Facilitate Sharing Cell Phone Distress Location Data with the Coast Guard

Interviewees suggested that a significant proportion of distress calls received and communications with mariners in distress do not include location information, whether those are 911 calls from which location information is not shared or direct calls made with cell phones. For instance, the private use of land lines, or wire lines, will continue to decrease as cell phone technology, affordability, and reliability improve and as the public increasingly relies on cellular communications.[1] Yet location information for those in distress is often not available, which constrains the USCG's ability to assist those in need. Developing procedures that enable people to share their GPS locations from their cell phones when they are in distress could help to remedy this. In some cases, these procedures can be as simple as emphasizing existing ways to share locations. For instance, the USCG could highlight these methods in existing outreach to the boating public. It could also develop procedures for its operation centers that would run through these possibilities with the caller, increasing the likelihood that the location could be shared in some way. The USCG could also seek to accelerate implementation of next-generation 911 systems, which would receive messages by text, and could share these advances with other first responders (Gallagher, 2018).

Among several location-sharing options described in the rest of this section are messaging and mapping options that the USCG could implement; these rely on apps that people probably already have. The other options—developing a dedicated app and developing a web browser capability—should be considered for the longer term; they would require some resources to implement. These solutions should also seek to minimize bandwidth and power requirements. This could require obtaining approval for software that enables text messaging

---

[1]   Calls for SAR assistance routinely originate from wire lines for overdue-mariner cases and flare sightings; however, as more homeowners opt out of wire-line use, reporting via wire lines will likely decrease commensurately.

from computers so that the USCG could send messages to those who have called needing assistance, access to websites to which the most-common navigation apps (e.g., Google Maps) link so that USCG command centers could open links sent to it, and developing basic guides that people in the command center could use to walk callers through how to send locations.

Messaging Apps

Several widely used messaging apps, such as Facebook Messenger (Facebook, undated) and Google Hangouts (Google, undated), enable users to share their location with other users directly within the app. Some apps allow users to share locations for a specified period of time, thus enabling the USCG to see where a distressed party might have moved (i.e., drifted) before they could be reached. In case of an emergency, a user might have limited time or cell coverage, thus making it more likely that they could use apps with which they were familiar. As a result, if a device has these apps already, this type of location sharing would be relatively straightforward. The downside is that these solutions might require the USCG command center to have access to the same app as the person in distress and be able to tell them where to send the information. On the other hand, someone concerned about privacy might have turned off location services for messaging apps.

Mapping Apps

Several popular mapping apps (e.g., Apple Maps, Google Maps, Waze) allow a user to share a location to a messaging app or through text message. This option could be useful for emergency response for a few reasons. First, the adoption rate for map and navigation apps is high (Panko, 2018). Second, because location can be shared via text message, the USCG could ask the person needing assistance to reply to a text message that it would send. And someone with a navigation app would very likely have location services turned on for that app. However, this option requires more steps than some of the other options. It should be straightforward for those who have done it before, but it might be difficult for those unfamiliar with how to share their locations.

A Dedicated App

The USCG could create a dedicated app to allow communications with those in distress. With a well-designed app, sharing a location could be very easy. This could seek to build on existing public-facing response organization apps, such as the USCG recreational boating safety app that a private foundation provided to the USCG and released in 2015. The USCG's app has large, red "emergency assistance" buttons on every view in the app. The app is intended to supplement—not replace—a VHF radio, providing boating safety tips and an emergency call button. When location services are enabled on the device and in the app, pressing the button has the app contact the closest USCG command center.

The existing app can be improved in several low-cost ways. First, uptake has been poor. We did not obtain download numbers from the USCG, but the USCG app has received approximately 5 percent as many user reviews on app download stores as Sea Tow, a maritime safety app that connects to a private marine assistance provider, has. Furthermore, few marinas promote or recommend using the app. This suggests low interest in the application. Second, the app's functionality could be improved. The user interface places the emergency call button too close to other functions, increasing the likelihood of accidentally requesting assistance. Recommendations from SMEs about how to improve a dedicated app included allowing a permanent user profile in which a mariner could describe their boat, easier ability to log float plans, an option to share float plans with friends and family and through social media, and improved access to marine support (e.g., emergency response, weather, tidal conditions). Promotion of the use of the app could be propagated through Marine Transportation System user outreach by the USCG Auxiliary during its boating safety schools; through national and state safe-boating campaigns; and through ongoing local USCG station engagements with maritime organizations, recreational boating and fishing associations, and yachting communities. Finally, the app could add social features similar to those in radio communications, on which mariners can talk with the USCG and other mariners. If a mariner is in a situation that is not immediately critical (e.g., a disabled vessel), the mariner could use the app's social features to communicate and potentially get assistance from other mariners or commercial marine assistance companies, thus reducing the burden on the USCG.

To identify the desired functionality, the USCG could review other apps, such as Sea Tow, that have push-button capability to request emergency and nonemergency support. However, devoting resources to developing a dedicated app that bridges radio, voice, and social media channels and that could facilitate distress calls might have some downsides. Specifically, the adoption of limited-use apps can be low in general, and the adoption rate for the USCG app appears to be extremely low. Because the USCG would need to invest in initial development and subsequent updates, the benefits might not justify the needed resources. An alternative could be to work to connect with other water-centric apps. Other water activities (e.g., surfing, kayaking, rafting, paddleboarding) have apps that could allow or already have an emergency feature, such as Paddle Logger's Paddler in Trouble. A final option to explore is the uptake of GPS-enabled, waterproof, and sometimes cellular-capable wearables that could offer another avenue to share one's location.

Web Browsers

Allowing mariners to share locations through web browsers could be the most universal and usable solution. The USCG could text a website link to a mariner in distress. Clicking that link would open a browser with a single button sharing the user's location with the USCG. Doing so might require more up-front investment and development than messaging and mapping apps would, but it could require fewer resources than a dedicated app would.

Recommendation 2: Ensure That an Organization Assumes Responsibility for Understanding Cell Coverage over Water

Cell phones have become crucial to the USCG SAR mission. Identifying the means that people can and will use to share their location would be one way to help. Another way to help ensure that the USCG is prepared for trends in how people communicate is ensuring that cellular coverage is available over water. However, the USCG has no responsibility or insight into what current cellular coverage is or what long-term risks exist in relying on cellular phones for the SAR mission.

As a result, the USCG does not have reliable information about the presence of cellular coverage over bodies of water, either to inform its own missions or to share with mariners. The FCC has oversight responsibility for cellular coverage in the United States, at least on land. Whether this authority extends to water is unclear because cellular coverage maps do not include areas over water. The USCG bears responsibility for maintaining certain radio frequencies and systems a certain distance from shore, but it does not appear that any organization is specifically responsible for monitoring, overseeing, or advocating cellular coverage over water.

This lack of specific responsibility can have important implications for any missions that could depend on the availability of cellular communications. As next-generation (e.g., 5G) cellular networks proliferate, there is no guarantee that cellular coverage over water will improve if those networks focus their coverage areas on land. Moreover, 5G networks will have smaller cells, which could lead to less "spillover" coverage over water.

The USCG could seek to directly collect coverage information by conducting tests of cell phone signals at different distances from shore at deployed assets. Filling in knowledge gaps in this manner would also allow the USCG to tailor coverage maps that would cover regions that were important to its mission.

The USCG should also consider advocating that it or another organization be responsible for maintaining oversight of cellular coverage over water. Future analysis of overwater cellular coverage should consider economic trade-offs between investments in cellular coverage over U.S. territorial water and those in radio. For example, the USCG could consider subsidizing cell phone companies to provide coverage over bodies of water, similar to subsidies available to carriers for providing rural coverage.

Recommendation 3: Identify Additional Uses of Social Media for Other Coast Guard Missions

The USCG could seek to identify other missions for which social media information could help increase maritime safety and security and enhance environmental protection and response operations (e.g., reporting environmental hazards, such as oil spills). Although the primary focus of this research was the USCG's response operations, the findings and recommendations could hold benefits for other USCG mission sets, such as prevention-oriented missions; for example, the USCG's prevention operations include marine safety (inspections, investigations, and waterway management). Identifying additional missions for which social media would be useful could help bolster the case for investments in developing guidance and capabilities for response operations. Social media capabilities could be useful in supporting marine casualty investigations and civil investigations relating to this regulatory mission, which the USCG considers a prevention mission rather than response operations. Passive monitoring of social media activity could help the USCG gain awareness of potential regulatory noncompliance or social interest in an event affecting maritime safety or security (e.g., protests, facility strikes, large marine events).

Future Work

In this research, we explored ways in which social media are being used to provide situational awareness in disaster response and sought to identify potential challenges that the USCG might face in carrying out such missions. We anticipate that further research on this topic could benefit other DHS components that conduct response operations, such as FEMA and the U.S. Secret Service. For instance, such additional research could do the following:

- Inform new or modified policies on how DHS should use social media aggregation or information extraction tools in response operations.

- Develop acquisition requirements for social media aggregation or information extraction tools to aid in response operations.
- Examine the potential roles of social media in DHS operations beyond response operations.
- Evaluate the current use of social media for information dissemination during response operations and whether such dissemination could be made more efficient or effective.

Interview Protocol

This appendix provides a copy of the interview protocol used in our research.

Does your organization currently use information from social media or monitor social media during response operations?

If organization does use social media, ask these questions:

- How is monitoring of social media done?
- What is the standard workflow for checking social media?
- How frequently do you check social media?
- Which social media platforms do you monitor?
- Do you have policies or structures in place to handle cybersecurity risks?
- Do you have policies or structures in place to evaluate the quality of information to combat potential disinformation on social media?

Do you currently use any tools to facilitate social media monitoring (e.g., social media aggregators)?

If yes,

- Which tools are you using?
- What do you like about these tools?
- What gaps in functionality, if any, have you experienced?

If no,

- Why not?
- Have you heard of tools that may be relevant to your mission? What are they?

In what ways (if any) are your current methods for monitoring social media working well?

- What metrics do you use to assess this?

In what ways (if any) are your current methods for monitoring social media during response operations not working well?

- What metrics do you use to assess this?

If the organization does not use social media, ask these questions:

- Have you ever used social media in this way? If yes, why did you stop?
- Why does your organization not monitor social media during response operations? (Ask about barriers or relevance to mission or particular use cases.)
- Have you heard of tools that may be relevant to your mission?

Are there other organizations similar to yours that you know do use social media in this way?

Ask all:

What types of capabilities (if any) do you think would be useful in a tool to monitor social media during response operations?

Analysis of Marine Information for Safety and Law Enforcement Data

This appendix provides more detail on our analysis of MISLE data.

The Coast Guard's Search-and-Rescue Workflow

Each time the USCG receives a distress call or is asked to render assistance when someone or something is at risk of injury or loss, the USCG opens a SAR case in the MISLE system (USCG, 2013). Generally, SAR operations move through five stages: awareness, initial action, planning, operation, and conclusion. During the awareness and initial action stages, the USCG gathers and records details about the case, such as the type of incident (e.g., person in water, vessel run aground), estimated location, and method of notification (e.g., R21, telephone, 911). If the USCG deploys a resource (e.g., cutter, helicopter) to respond to a case, it logs one sortie for each asset deployed in resolving the case.[1] At the case's conclusion, the USCG records the results of any sortie and any information on loss of life and damage to property.

What We Did

We acquired one file per fiscal year for 2012 through 2018 of cases recorded in the USCG MISLE system. We read each file into a data

---

[1] A sortie is an "[i]ndividual movement of a resource in conducting a search or rendering assistance" (National SAR Committee, 2018, p. xlvi).

frame, in which we filtered the data to consist of only SAR cases, then cleaned and concatenated the data into one file for all years. We exported the data into ArcGIS, in which we mapped all cases. To classify cases based on distance from shore, we used the buffer tool to create three different-sized ranges from the boundaries of the United States:[2] 3 nm, capturing cases that occurred within the area of state/federal concurrent jurisdiction; 12 nm, capturing cases that occurred within U.S. territorial waters; and 24 nm, capturing cases that occurred within the U.S. customs contiguous zone.

Separately, we acquired a data set of locations of cellular towers from the Homeland Infrastructure Foundation-Level Data project (Homeland Infrastructure Foundation-Level Data, 2017), which we overlaid in ArcGIS, along with the MISLE case data. Using the buffer tool, we created a 20-mile radius around each tower location. We used this to construct Figure 3.1 in Chapter Three, the map of SAR cases in southern Florida in FY 2018. In addition to the base map, we included three polygon layers (one to indicate each important zone surrounding the shore) and created four separate point layers to show locations of SAR cases: (1) those reported via cell phone in which lives were lost, (2) those reported via cell phone in which no lives were lost, (3) those reported via all other methods in which lives were lost, and (4) those reported via all other methods in which no lives were lost.

Despite having access to the Homeland Infrastructure Foundation-Level Data, we decided to remove cell tower buffer zones from the published maps and analyses because we were unable to arrive at range estimates based on a validated model from the scientific literature. Like VHF radio technology, cellular communication involves waves that are part of the radio spectrum and require line of sight to transmit a signal from tower to device. Because of this, cellular tower range can vary based on surrounding terrain (e.g., hills, mountains, forests), built infrastructure (e.g., height of tower, presence or absence of tall or densely packed buildings), and weather (e.g., clouds, precipitation, wind, shade). The FCC publishes a map of overland Long-Term Evolution coverage, but we were unable to find a shapefile to include in our

---

[2]   We included Alaska and Hawaii but excluded small barrier islands.

analysis; we were also unable to locate any documentation of the model the FCC uses to estimate tower range for that map.

What We Found

Overall, we found a total of 120,371 total cases from FYs 2012 through 2018. Of those, 81,740 (67.9 percent) occurred less than or equal to 3 nm from the shore; an additional 13,963 were between 3 and 12 nm from shore; 4,244 were between 12 and 24 nm from shore; and the remaining 20,424 cases were either missing a coded location or occurred more than 24 nm from the shore. Around 84.5 percent of cases were within 20 miles of a cell tower.

Of the total cases, roughly 10.3 percent (12,485 cases) were confirmed to be reported to the USCG via cell phone; in addition, 31.2 percent of cases (37,567) were reported via telephone, but the data did not distinguish between calls from cell phones and those from wire lines. Table B.1 provides our findings.

Table B.1
Percentage of Calls Made from Cell Phones, by Originating Coast Guard District and Year

| District | Total Cases | Percentage of Calls | | | | | | | |
		2012	2013	2014	2015	2016	2017	2018	All
7	27,269	11.5	10.7	10.7	10.4	6.6	5.4	8.6	9.4
9	17,753	11.5	8.3	9.5	10.4	11.5	16.4	14.7	11.9
1	15,819	4.6	6.3	11.0	9.7	5.3	6.5	5.9	7.0
11	14,617	15.2	11.1	10.9	16.4	10.5	8.6	7.7	11.7
8	13,952	17.7	19.2	18.3	20.6	13.3	16.9	12.9	17.1
5	12,278	11.3	13.6	8.5	10.0	9.2	10.1	9.7	10.4
13	10,849	13.0	11.7	8.7	7.2	4.3	3.7	8.2	8.2
14	4,078	5.6	8.3	10.0	9.9	9.7	9.9	8.4	8.8
17	3,751	8.4	10.6	11.7	6.1	8.1	6.1	6.5	8.2

References

911.gov, "Public Safety Information on 'Swatting,'" May 2015. As of November 5, 2019:
https://www.911.gov/pdf/
National_911_Program_Public_Safety_Information_Swatting_2015.pdf

American Red Cross, "More Americans Using Mobile Apps in Emergencies," press release, August 31, 2012. As of November 5, 2019:
https://www.prnewswire.com/news-releases/
more-americans-using-mobile-apps-in-emergencies-168144726.html

Beath, Cynthia, Irma Becerra-Fernandez, Jeanne Ross, and James Short, "Finding Value in the Information Explosion," *MIT Sloan Management Review*, Vol. 53, No. 4, Summer 2012, pp. 17–20. As of December 9, 2019:
https://sloanreview.mit.edu/article/finding-value-in-the-information-explosion/

DHS—*See* U.S. Department of Homeland Security.

Facebook, "How Do I Share My Live Location in Messenger?" undated. As of November 5, 2019:
https://www.facebook.com/help/messenger-app/1256099024444800

FCC—*See* Federal Communications Commission.

Federal Communications Commission, "Nationwide LTE Coverage: YE 2017," updated December 21, 2018. As of November 5, 2019:
https://www.fcc.gov/reports-research/maps/nationwide-lte-coverage-ye-2017/

Federal Emergency Management Agency, "Emergency Support Function Annexes," updated October 29, 2019a. As of November 5, 2019:
https://www.fema.gov/media-library/assets/documents/25512

———, "National Preparedness Resource Library," updated October 29, 2019b. As of November 5, 2019:
https://www.fema.gov/national-preparedness-resource-library

FEMA—*See* Federal Emergency Management Agency.

Gallagher, Jill C., "Next Generation 911 Technologies: Select Issues for Congress," Washington, D.C.: Congressional Research Service, R45253, version 4, July 9, 2018. As of November 5, 2019:
https://crsreports.congress.gov/product/details?prodcode=R45253

Google, "Share Your Photos, Videos, or Location," *Hangouts Help*, undated. As of October 2019:
https://support.google.com/hangouts/answer/3115410?co=GENIE.Platform%3DAndroid&hl=en

Homeland Infrastructure Foundation-Level Data, "Cellular Towers," 2017. Current version, as of November 5, 2019:
https://hifldgeoplatform.opendata.arcgis.com/datasets/0835ba2ed38f494196c14af8407454fb_0

Kiron, David, Pamela Kirk Prentice, and Renee Boucher Ferguson, *The Analytics Mandate: Findings from the 2014 Data and Analytics Global Executive Study and Research Report, Massachusetts Institute of Technology Sloan Management Review* Research Report, May 12, 2014. As of December 9, 2019:
https://sloanreview.mit.edu/projects/analytics-mandate/

Landwehr, Peter M., Wei Wei, Michael Kowalchuck, and Kathleen M. Carley, "Using Tweets to Support Disaster Planning, Warning and Response," *Safety Science*, Vol. 90, December 2016, pp. 33–47.

Marcellino, William, Meagan L. Smith, Christopher Paul, and Lauren Skrabala, *Monitoring Social Media: Lessons for Future Department of Defense Social Media Analysis in Support of Information Operations*, Santa Monica, Calif.: RAND Corporation, RR-1742-OSD, 2017. As of November 5, 2019:
https://www.rand.org/pubs/research_reports/RR1742.html

McKinney, Earl H., "Supporting Pre-Existing Teams in Crisis with IT: A Preliminary Organizational-Team Collaboration Framework," *Journal of Information Technology Theory and Application*, Vol. 9, No. 3, 2009, pp. 39–59.

Moroney, Jennifer D. P., Stephanie Pezard, Laurel E. Miller, Jeffrey Engstrom, and Abby Doll, *Lessons from Department of Defense Disaster Relief Efforts in the Asia–Pacific Region*, Santa Monica, Calif.: RAND Corporation, RR-146-OSD, 2013. As of November 5, 2019:
https://www.rand.org/pubs/research_reports/RR146.html

National Emergency Number Association, "9-1-1 Statistics," undated. As of October 2019:
https://www.nena.org/page/911Statistics

National SAR Committee—*See* National Search and Rescue Committee.

National Search and Rescue Committee, *United States National Search and Rescue Supplement to the International Aeronautical and Maritime Search and Rescue Manual*, version 2.0, April 23, 2018. As of November 5, 2019:
https://www.dco.uscg.mil/Our-Organization/
Assistant-Commandant-for-Response-Policy-CG-5R/
Office-of-Incident-Management-Preparedness-CG-5RI/
US-Coast-Guard-Office-of-Search-and-Rescue-CG-SAR/SAR-Publications/

Office of the Chief of Public Affairs, Online and Social Media Division, U.S. Army, *U.S. Army Social Media Handbook*, Washington, D.C., January 2011. As of November 5, 2019:
https://apps.dtic.mil/dtic/tr/fulltext/u2/a549468.pdf

Panko, Riley, "The Popularity of Google Maps: Trends in Navigation Apps in 2018," *The Manifest*, July 10, 2018. As of November 5, 2019:
https://themanifest.com/app-development/
popularity-google-maps-trends-navigation-apps-2018

Pew Research Center, "Social Media Fact Sheet," June 12, 2019. As of November 5, 2019:
http://www.pewinternet.org/fact-sheet/social-media/

Porter, T. J., "Remote Support: A Crucial Part of TR Operations," Team Rubicon Disaster Response, September 6, 2018. As of November 5, 2019:
https://teamrubiconusa.org/blog/remote-support-a-crucial-part-of-tr-operations/

Public Law 107-296, Homeland Security Act of 2002, November 25, 2002. As of May 12, 2019:
https://www.govinfo.gov/app/details/PLAW-107publ296

Reuter, Christian, and Marc-André Kaufhold, "Fifteen Years of Social Media in Emergencies: A Retrospective Review and Future Directions for Crisis Informatics," *Journal of Contingencies and Crisis Management*, Vol. 26, No. 1, March 2018, pp. 41–57.

Tim, Yenni, Shan L. Pan, Peter Ractham, and Laddawan Kaewkitipong, "Digitally Enabled Disaster Response: The Emergence of Social Media as Boundary Objects in a Flooding Disaster," *Information Systems Journal*, Vol. 27, No. 2, March 2017, pp. 197–232.

U.S. Coast Guard, *U.S. Coast Guard Addendum to the United States National Search and Rescue Supplement (NSS) to the International Aeronautical and Maritime Search and Rescue Manual (IAMSAR)*, Commandant Instruction M16130.2F, January 2013. As of November 5, 2019:
https://www.hsdl.org/?abstract&did=748220

———, Office of Performance Management and Assessment, *Search and Rescue Mission Analysis Report*, September 5, 2019.

U.S. Code, Title 6, Domestic Security; Chapter 1, Homeland Security Organization; Subchapter III, Science and Technology in Support of Homeland Security; Section 185, Federally Funded Research and Development Centers. As of May 12, 2019:
https://www.govinfo.gov/app/details/USCODE-2017-title6/
USCODE-2017-title6-chap1-subchapIII-sec185

U.S. Department of Homeland Security, "Emergency Support Function #9: Search and Rescue Annex," annex to the National Response Framework, June 2016. As of November 5, 2019:
https://www.fema.gov/media-library/assets/documents/25512

———, "Privacy Policy for Operational Use of Social Media," Instruction 110-01-001, revision 0, June 8, 2012. As of November 5, 2019:
https://www.dhs.gov/publication/
privacy-policy-operational-use-social-media-instruction-110-01-001#

———, *Countering False Information on Social Media in Disasters and Emergencies: Social Media Working Group for Emergency Services and Disaster Management*, March 2018. As of November 5, 2019:
https://www.dhs.gov/sites/default/files/publications/SMWG_Countering-False-Info-Social-Media-Disasters-Emergencies_Mar2018-508.pdf

U.S. Government Accountability Office, *Coast Guard: Actions Needed to Close Stations Identified as Overlapping and Unnecessarily Duplicative*, GAO-18-9, October 26, 2017. As of November 5, 2019:
https://www.gao.gov/Products/GAO-18-9

USCG—*See* U.S. Coast Guard.